SING A
OF ANIMALS

Written and Compiled by **Durby Peterson** and **Jean Warren**
Illustrated by **Kelly McMahon**

Totline® Publications
A Division of Frank Schaffer Publications, Inc.
Torrance, California

Totline Publications would like to thank the following people for their contributions to this book: Pat Beck, Red Lion, PA; Terri Crosbie, Oldwick, NJ; Cindy Dingwall, Palatine, IL; Judy Hall, Wytheville, VA; Debra Lindahl, Libertyville, IL; Susan A. Miller, Kutztown, PA; Susan M. Paprocki, Northbrook, IL; Susan Peters, Upland, CA; Barbara Robinson, Glendale, AZ; Sue Schliecker, Waukesha, WI; Betty Silkunas, Lansdale, PA; Carla Cotter Skjong, Tyler, MN; Becky Valenick, Rockford, IL; Bonnie Woodard, Bossier City, LA.

Managing Editor: Kathleen Cubley
Contributing Editors: Carol Gnojewski, Susan Hodges, Elizabeth McKinnon
Copyeditor: Kris Fulsaas
Proofreader: Miriam Bulmer
Graphic Designer: Sarah Ness
Layout Artist: Laura Horman
Graphic Designer (Cover): Brenda Mann Harrison
Cover Illustrator: Janet McDonnell
Production Manager: Melody Olney

Some of the ideas in this book may appear in other Totline® publications.

ISBN: 1-57029-168-3

Printed in the United States of America
Published by Totline® Publications
Editorial Office: P.O. Box 2250
Everett, WA 98203
Business Office: 23740 Hawthorne Blvd.
Torrance, CA 90505

20 19 18 17 16 15 14 13 12 11 10 9 8 7 6 5 4 3 2 1

INTRODUCTION

Sing a song with your child, and several great things happen: you have a merry time together, your child learns, and you pass along a love for music.

Songs play a unique role in helping young children learn. Involvement in music develops listening skills, nurtures creativity, and builds memory power. The fun word play and repetition of sounds within songs increase your child's vocabulary and inspire a love for language. Enjoying silly songs together also encourages a child's developing sense of humor.

Sing a Song of Animals is divided into seven chapters, each one inviting your child to explore a different part of the animal kingdom. Begin your musical adventure with the animals most familiar, and continue on to discover those most exotic or far away. As you go, sing of animals at home, on the farm, in the meadow, in the forest, in the ocean, and at the zoo. The songs are written to the tunes of childhood favorites, making them easy to sing. Next to each song is an age-appropriate activity designed to extend the fun of meeting each animal. You will easily incorporate singing into your daily routines as you and your child venture forth into the fascinating world of animals.

Singing is fun to do any time, so why not start right now? Just open the book, choose a song with its related activity, and enjoy making music with your child!

A WORD ABOUT SAFETY—All the activities in this book are appropriate for young children. However, it is important that an adult supervise the activities to make sure that children do not put any materials or objects in their mouth. As for art materials, such as scissors, glue, or felt tip markers, use those that are specifically labeled as safe for children unless the materials are to be used only by an adult.

CONTENTS

YOUR PUPPY

Sung to: "Skip to My Lou"

Walk, walk, walk your puppy.
Walk, walk, walk your puppy.
Walk, walk, walk your puppy.
Safely along the street.

Brush, brush, brush your puppy.
Brush, brush, brush your puppy.
Brush, brush, brush your puppy.
Make puppy clean and neat.

Feed, feed, feed your puppy.
Feed, feed, feed your puppy.
Feed, feed, feed your puppy.
Puppies need food to eat.

Cindy Dingwall

Sing "Your Puppy" and talk with your child about pet care. If you have a dog, encourage her to give it food, water, and, of course, lots of love. Show her how you brush and exercise the dog. If you don't have a dog, let her practice with a stuffed animal or two.

MY PET GOLDFISH

Sung to: "The Muffin Man"

Have you seen my pet goldfish,

My pet goldfish,

My pet goldfish?

Have you seen my pet goldfish?

He stays in water all day.

He likes to swim around and round,

Around and round,

Around and round.

He likes to swim around and round,

Because he likes to play.

It is my job to give him food,

To give him food,

To give him food.

It is my job to give him food;

I feed him every day.

Jean Warren

Help your child make something fishy for his wall. Invite him to help you tear up a sheet of orange construction paper into small pieces. Then cut a large goldfish shape out of white construction paper and spread it with glue. Invite your child to stick the orange "scales" all over his fish.

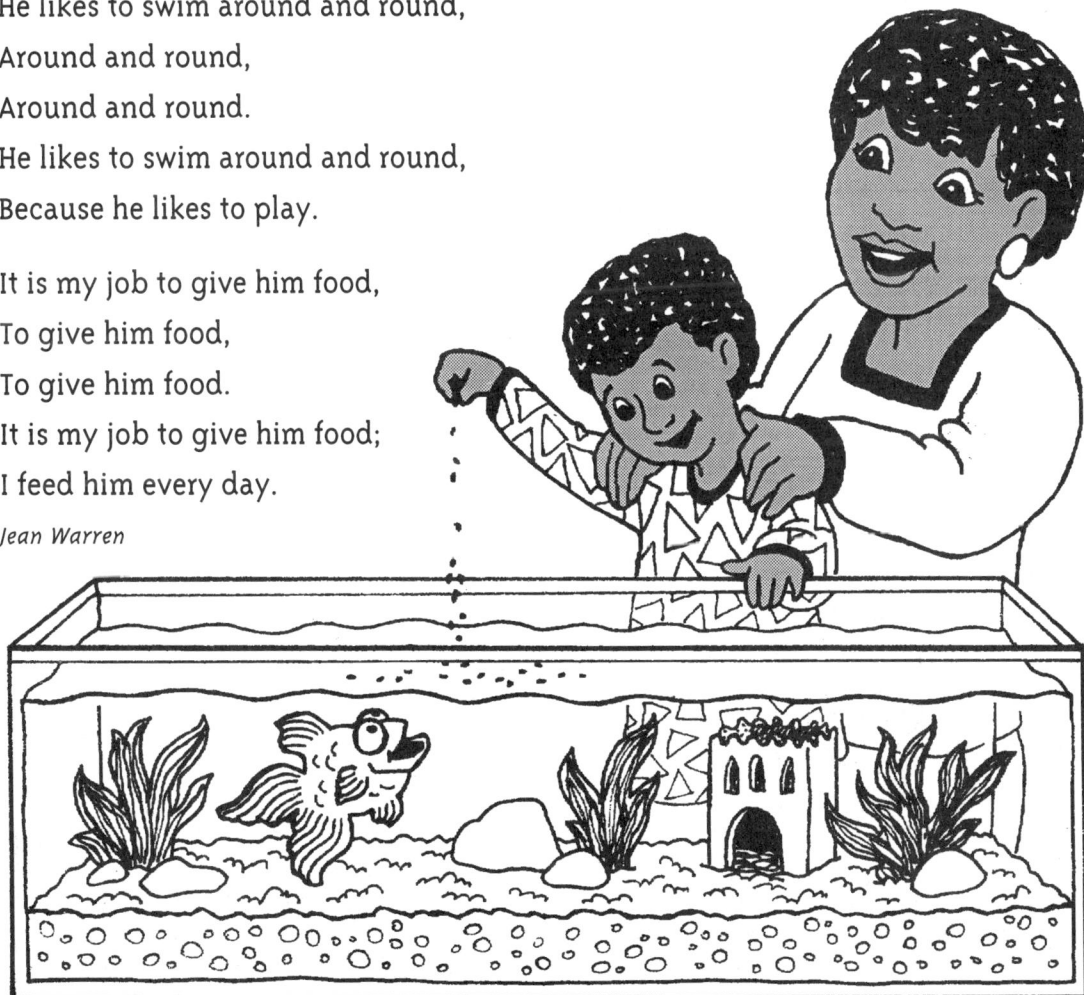

WHO AM I?

Sung to: "Twinkle, Twinkle, Little Star"

Soft fur, paws, and small pink nose—
Do you know who has all those?
Pretty whiskers, fluffy tail,
Tongue that laps milk from a pail—
Would you like to take a guess?
Did you say a kitten? Yes!

Becky Valenick

After singing "Who Am I?" make up other animal riddles and let your child guess who you are. You might ask, "What animal is slow and carries his house?" or "What animal has long ears and a fluffy white tail?" Encourage your child to make up her own animal riddles.

I'M A LITTLE TURTLE

Sung to: "I'm a Little Teapot"

I'm a little turtle right at home.

From my house I never roam.

If I have to move, I never pack.

My home is always on my back.

Jean Warren

Give your child a turtle for a snacktime treat. Slice an apple in half vertically and place it (cut side down) on a plate to form the shell. Let the stem be the turtle's tail. Cut a slice of cheese into 4 strips and arrange them for the feet. Use a banana round for the head, with two raisin eyes on top.

DOWN BY THE FARMHOUSE

Sung to: "Down by the Station"

Down by the farmhouse, early in the morning,
See the chicken family pecking in a row.
See the mommy chicken, she is called a hen.
Cluck, cluck, cluck, and
Off she goes.

Down by the farmhouse, early in the morning,
See the chicken family pecking in a row.
See the daddy chicken, he is called a rooster.
Cock-a-doodle-doo and
Off he goes.

Down by the farmhouse, early in the morning,
See the chicken family pecking in a row.
See the baby chickens, they are called chicks.
Peep, peep, peep, and
Off they go.

Carla Cotter Skjong

After singing "Down by the Farmhouse" together, help your child learn the names of other animal parents and their young. Teach her names such as bull, cow, and calf; gander, goose, and gosling; and so forth. She will be intrigued to discover so many different animal names.

THIS LITTLE LAMB

Sung to: "Twinkle, Twinkle, Little Star"

This little lamb eats grass and hay.
This little lamb just likes to play.
This little lamb drinks water cool.
This little lamb runs off to school.
This little lamb just wants to stay
And wag its little tail all day.

Jean Warren

Give your child a feel for the farm with this sensory activity. Cut a simple lamb shape out of thin cardboard such as a cereal box. Set out cotton balls and glue. Let your youngster dip the cotton balls into the glue and stick them onto the lamb. Explain that sheep's wool is sheared every spring for use in making warm clothing.

ALL AROUND THE BARNYARD

Sung to: "Pop! Goes the Weasel"

All around the barnyard today,
    (Sing first verse quietly.)

The animals are asleep—

The cows and horses, pigs and sheep.

Shhh, don't make a peep.

Here comes the rooster, bold and proud,
    (Sing second verse loudly.)

To sound his daily alarm.

Cock-a-doodle-doodle-doo,

Cock-a-doodle-doo.

Pat Beck

Your child's stuffed animals have a special part in this activity. Have her place them around a pretend "barnyard." Invite her to make believe it is very early morning and all the animals are fast asleep. She can play the part of the rooster who crows and wakes up all the other farm animals.

DOWN ON THE FARM

Sung to: "On Top of Old Smokey"

A pig and a rooster,
A cow in the barn
Are waiting to meet us
Back down on the farm.

A goat or a chicken,
And sometimes a mouse,
Will be there to greet us
Beside the farmhouse.

Bonnie Woodard

Bring this song to life with a simple felt farm. Cut a large barn shape out of red felt. Give your barn a cutout door. Place the barn on a table or flannelboard. From other colors of felt, cut out one each of the animals mentioned in "Down on the Farm." Your child can play the farmer moving the animals about the barnyard.

FLITTER, FLITTER, BUTTERFLY

Sung to: "Skip to My Lou"

Flitter, flitter, butterfly.
Flitter, flitter, butterfly.
Flitter, flitter, butterfly.
I see you flitting by.

Flutter, flutter, butterfly.
Flutter, flutter, butterfly.
Flutter, flutter, butterfly.
You make me want to fly.

Jean Warren

Give your child a chance to try her own butterfly wings. Using two scarves, pin one end of each scarf onto her clothing at the shoulders. Loosely pin the other ends around each of her wrists. Tell your youngster she is in a meadow, fluttering over the flowers. As you sing "Flitter, Flitter, Butterfly," she will enjoy dancing around the room or yard.

DID YOU EVER SEE A FROG?

Sung to: "Did You Ever See a Lassie?"

Did you ever see a frog,

A frog, a frog?

Did you ever see a frog

Jump this way and that?

Jump this way

And that way.

Jump this way

And that way.

Did you ever see a frog

Jump this way and that?

Additional verses: Substitute *hop, croak,* and *leap* for *jump.*

Adapted Traditional

Turn your living room into a meadow pond and let your child be the frog. Lay some pillows or cushions all around on the floor. Explain that they are lily pads floating in a giant pond. As you sing "Did You Ever See a Frog?" have him squat and then leap from one pillow to the next.

THE HONEYBEE

Sung to: "If You're Happy and You Know It"

Oh, the honeybee makes a little buzz
As she flies around doing what she does,
Sipping nectar from a flower,
Spreading pollen every hour.
Then she makes delicious honey,
Yes, she does!

Durby Peterson

Introduce your preschooler to the remarkable honeybee. Explain that bees gather nectar from flowers and use it to make delicious honey. As they gather nectar they also spread pollen from flower to flower, which is necessary for the production of fruits and vegetables. For a taste of the honeybee's handiwork, serve some honey on toast.

MEADOW MOUSE

Sung to: "Clementine"

In the meadow, in the meadow
Lives a little meadow mouse.
In the meadow, in the meadow,
In his little cozy house.

Just a bit of grass and fur
Or some feathers in a mound
Makes a snug bed for a mouse
In his home dug in the ground.

Just a seed or leaf or root,
Something small to nibble on,
Makes a nice meal for a mouse
In the meadow all day long.

Durby Peterson

Young children are fascinated by small creatures such as mice. After you sing "Meadow Mouse" with your child, let him nibble on some cheese as you read aloud your favorite version of "The Country Mouse and the City Mouse." Discuss the contrasts between the two mice in the story. Which mouse would your youngster rather be? Why?

I LIKE BIRDS

Sung to: "Three Blind Mice"

Birds, birds, birds.

Birds, birds, birds.

I like birds.

I like birds.

I like to watch how they build a nest.

I like the robins with bright red vests.

I like the chirp of the babies best.

Oh, I like birds.

Jean Warren

Your child will gain math skills with this homemade game. Make a bird's nest by rolling down the sides of a brown lunch bag. Let your child glue on small twigs and yarn pieces. Then give her some unshelled pecans to use for bird's eggs. Have your child roll a die and place that number of "eggs" in the nest.

Time for Sleeping

Sung to: "Sing a Song of Sixpence"

Now it's time for sleeping;
The bears go in their caves,
Keeping warm and cozy—
Time for lazy days.
When the snow is gone
And the sun comes out to play,
The bears wake from their slumber
And go along their way.

Terri Crosbie

At naptime, sing "Time for Sleeping" and have your youngster pretend to be a bear looking for a cave for his long winter's nap. Help him construct it with props such as a blanket draped over a card table or across two chairs in the corner. Then tuck him in with a big bear hug.

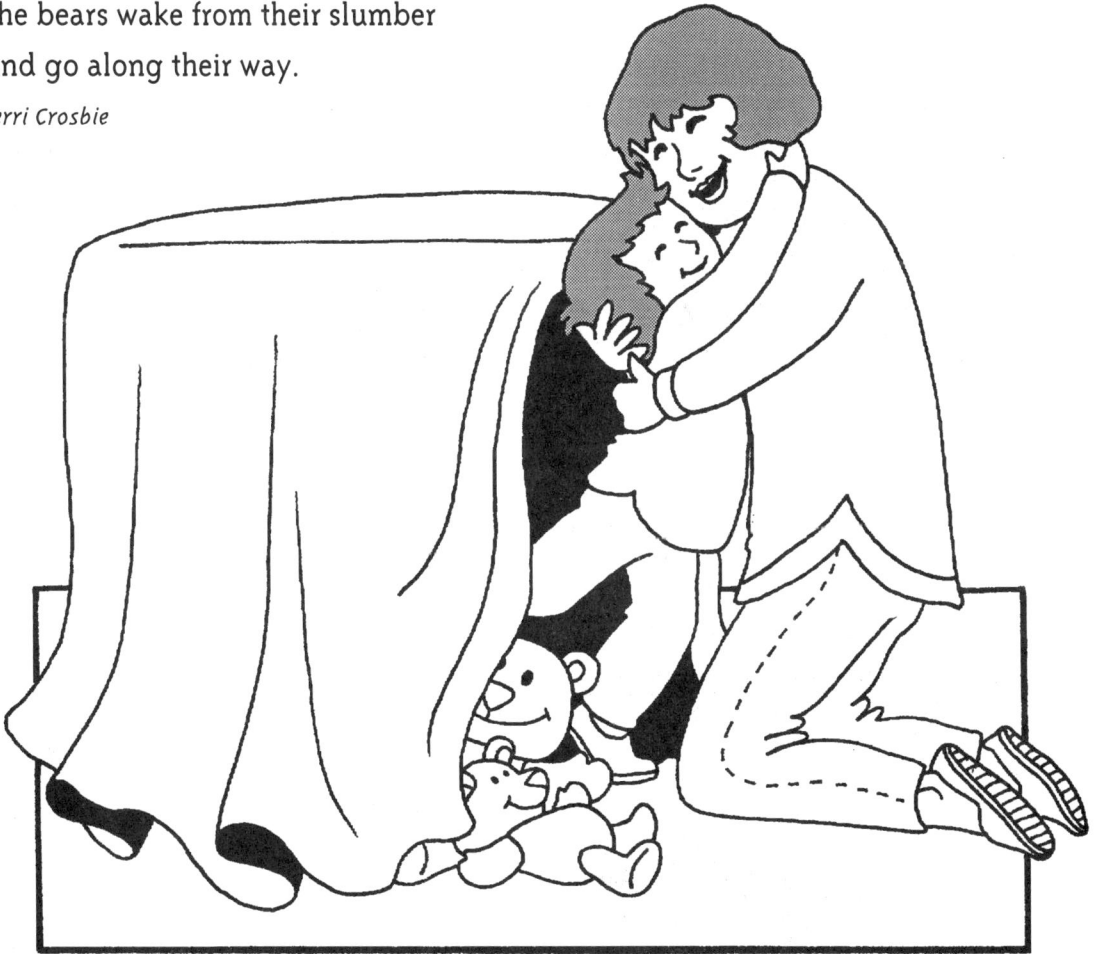

SEE THE FLUFFY RABBIT

Sung to: "I'm a Little Teapot"

See the fluffy rabbit as it hops,
One ear up while the other flops.
He's a gentle fellow with wiggly nose.
He's a ball of fur from his ears to his toes.

Susan M. Paprocki

Let the rabbit's example inspire your youngster to eat her vegetables. Share with your child the fact that rabbits enjoy tender bean sprouts, peas, carrots, and other fresh vegetables. Prepare a variety of chopped vegetables and have your child hop on over to the table to nibble a rabbit's snack.

Oh, Skunk

Sung to: "Oh Dear, What Can the Matter Be?"

Oh, oh, what is that awful smell?
Oh, oh, what is that awful smell?
Oh, oh, what is that awful smell?
A skunk's been here, I can tell.

Oh, skunk, why did you have to spray?
Oh, skunk, why did you have to spray?
Oh, skunk, why did you have to spray?
You make us all run away.

Susan Peters

Your child will be interested to hear that skunks protect themselves by spraying a smelly liquid when they are frightened or in danger. Explain that they give warning first by growling and stamping their feet, which makes them look angry. What does your child do when he is scared? What about when he is angry? What makes him feel scared or angry?

If You're Ever in a Forest

Sung to: "Did You Ever See a Lassie?"

If you're ever in a forest,
A forest, a forest,
If you're ever in a forest
You might see a deer.
They're gold as the sun.
They leap when they run.
If you're ever in a forest
You might see a deer.

Judy Hall

Your child will enjoy running and leaping like a deer with this activity. Find an open spot on the floor and set out some pillows for her to leap over. Tell her these are bushes and she is a deer running through the woods. Sing "If You're Ever in a Forest" as she runs, and her imagination will do the rest.

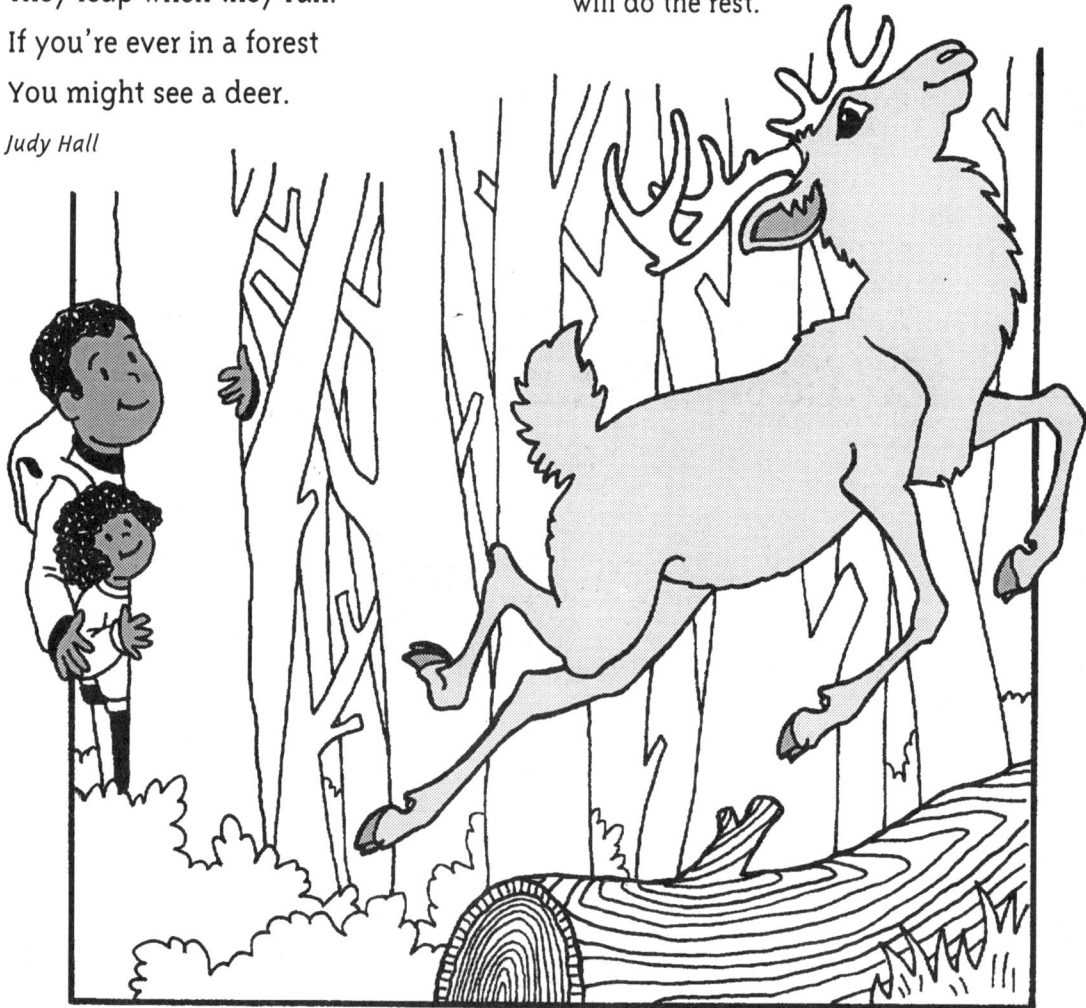

MR. OWL

Sung to: "Twinkle, Twinkle, Little Star"

Late at night when you're in bed,

Mr. Owl perks up his head.

He looks left and he looks right,

In the dark all through the night.

Hear him hoot when you're in bed.

Mr. Owl's no sleepyhead.

Betty Silkunas

An owl puppet can make nighttime seem more friendly. With a small paper sack folded flat, draw two large round eyes on the rectangle bottom. From construction paper, cut out a triangle beak and two small ears and tape them onto the sack. Let your child put the sack on his hand and fly Mr. Owl around the room, hooting good night to everyone.

THE SQUIRREL

Sung to: "The Farmer in the Dell"

The squirrel up in the tree,
The squirrel up in the tree—
Gray fur with a bushy tail,
The squirrel up in the tree.

The squirrel up in the tree,
The squirrel up in the tree,
He cracks some nuts and winks at me,
The squirrel up in the tree.

Bonnie Woodard

You can help your child develop counting and sorting skills with a pile of assorted hard-shell nuts from the grocery store. Have your child pretend to be a squirrel preparing for a long cold winter, and show her how to sort the nuts into different piles. Then help her count the nuts. Which pile has the most? The least?

HEY, RACCOON

Sung to: "Hickory, Dickory, Dock"

Hey, raccoon up in that tree,
You think you're fooling me.
Your mask is swell but I can see
You hiding up in that tree.

Bonnie Woodard

Share with your child the fact that raccoons are nocturnal animals. They stay up all night and sleep in their dens during the day. Darken your house and let your child move about as if searching for food. Then turn on the light and have him pretend to sleep. Repeat the cycle. Would he like to be a nocturnal animal?

I'm a Giant Blue Whale

Sung to: "I'm a Little Teapot"

I'm a giant blue whale, wild and free.
I leap from the ocean, I leap from the sea.
I spray lots of water from my spout.
Then I dive and swim about.

Carla Cotter Skjong

Share with your child the fact blue whales are the largest animals that have ever lived, including dinosaurs. They can grow up to 100 feet long. With your child, measure and mark off this distance outdoors. Help her to imagine an animal that large swimming alongside her.

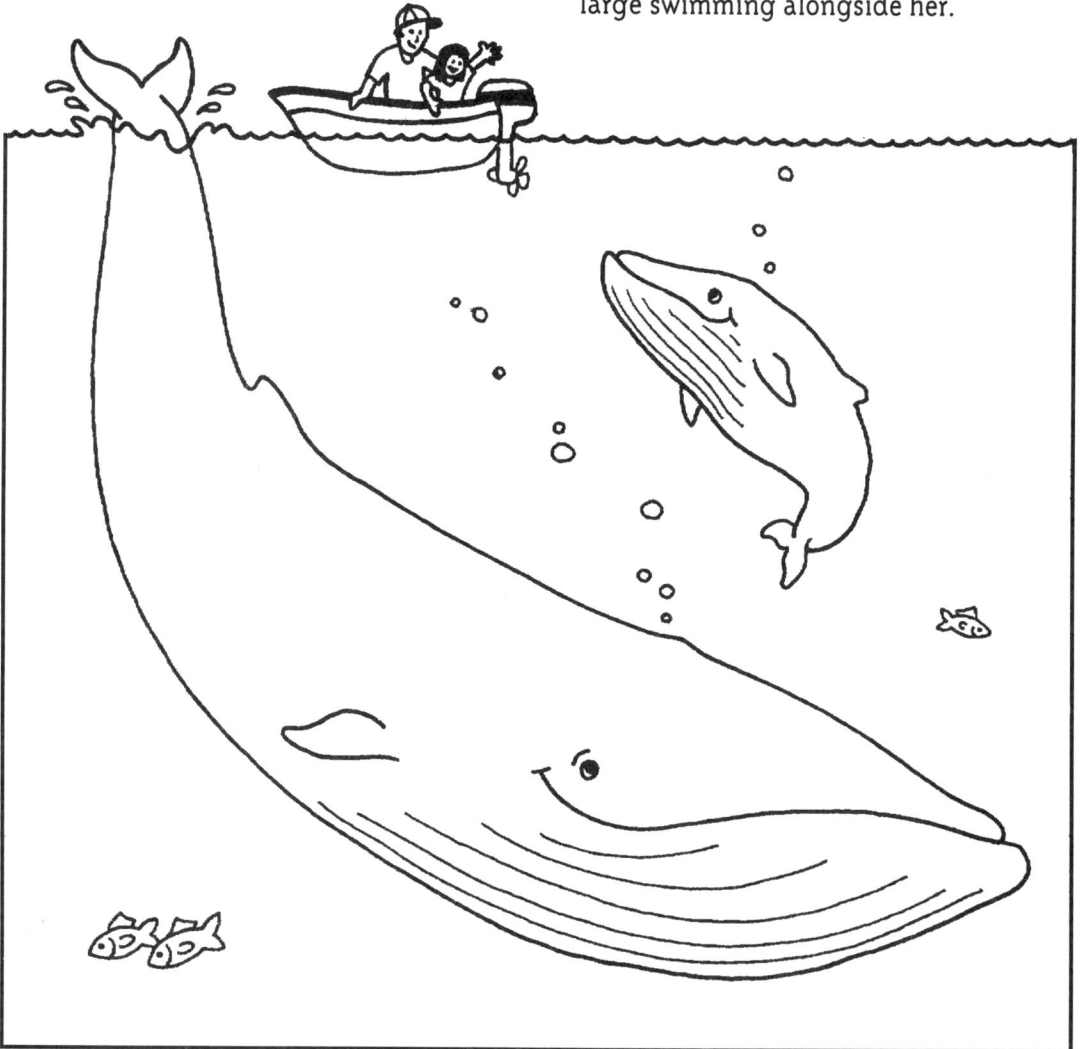

THE SHARK

Sung to: "She'll Be Coming Round the Mountain"

Oh, the shark has lots of really big sharp teeth.
Oh, the shark has lots of really big sharp teeth.
When his teeth fall out he grins
'Cause new teeth always grow in.
Oh, the shark has lots of really big sharp teeth.

Oh, the shark's big teeth can make him look so mean,
But I wonder if he keeps them very clean.
If he brushed them night and day
They might not fall out that way.
Oh, the shark's big teeth can make him look so mean.

Susan A. Miller

Explain to your child that a shark has several rows of teeth. When the old teeth fall out, a new row always grows in. Let your preschooler know that his baby teeth will fall out soon, to be replaced by permanent teeth, which are the last ones he will get. Have him pretend he's a shark who needs to brush. How would he like to have several rows of teeth to brush?

WE'RE BUSY LITTLE CRABS

Sung to: "The Farmer in the Dell"

We're busy little crabs
Who live down by the sea.
Everywhere we go, we run
As quick as quick can be.

We're busy little crabs
Who like to run and hide.
When you see us scooting by
It's always side to side.

Jean Warren

For an unusual movement activity, ask your child to pretend she's a crab down at the beach. Show her how to bend over and walk on her hands and feet. Can she maneuver sideways like a crab? If she has trouble, encourage her with the news that a crab has five pairs of legs, making its job a lot easier.

HAVE YOU EVER SEEN A SEA LION?

Sung to: "Did You Ever See a Lassie?"

Have you ever seen a sea lion, sea lion, sea lion?

Have you ever seen a sea lion make his flippers clap?

He claps and claps and claps and claps.

Have you ever seen a sea lion make his flippers clap?

Have you ever heard a sea lion, sea lion, sea lion?

Have you ever heard a sea lion go arf, arf, arf, arf?

He barks and barks and barks and barks.

Have you ever heard a sea lion go arf, arf, arf, arf?

Jean Warren

"Have You Ever Seen a Sea Lion?" is a great song for developing your child's sense of rhythm. Ask your youngster to help you keep the beat by clapping like a sea lion. Sing with a swinging, steady rhythm, clapping four times per line of the song. Repeat the song a few times and your child will know just what to do.

Sea Star

Sung to: "My Bonnie Lies Over the Ocean"

Oh, when I went down to the ocean,

I found a small star on the ground.

I thought stars belonged in the sky,

But this one was crawling around.

Sea star, sea star,

Crawling along on the beach, the beach.

Sea star, sea star,

You are a star I can reach!

Jean Warren

Your child will be seeing stars with this activity. On the back of a sheet of thin sandpaper, draw the shape of a sea star. Cut around it and repeat the process until you have about five sea stars. Hide them around your house and invite your child to go beach combing. How many sea stars can she find?

Mr. Octopus

Sung to: "Yankee Doodle"

Once I saw an octopus
Down in the deep, blue sea.
I called out, "Mr. Octopus,
Oh, won't you swim with me?"
He uncurled his tentacles,
Stretching them out straight.
One, two, three, four, five, six, seven,
I counted all eight!

Sue Schliecker

Give your child an octopus of his own. On a sheet of construction paper, draw seven parallel lines an equal distance apart. Cut along the lines about two thirds of the way up the paper. Roll the uncut portion of the paper into a tube and tape it together, with the cut strips dangling below. Draw a smiling face on the octopus's head and let your child bend the legs out in all directions, counting as he goes.

I Know a Giraffe

Sung to: "On Top of Old Smokey"

I know a giraffe,

She holds her head high.

She stretches and stretches

Her neck to the sky.

She lives on the plains

With elephants, too.

You also might see her

When you're at the zoo.

Judy Hall

Sing "I Know a Giraffe" with your child as you do some stretching exercises together. Ask her to see how high she can reach with her arms and how low she can bend over. Show your child how to sit with legs straight on the floor and reach for her toes. Can she imagine stretching her neck up to the trees?

GIRAFFE

WHAT A NOSE!

Sung to: "I'm a Little Teapot"

Elephants are big and tall and fat
They sway their trunks both this way and that.
Elephants have big ears and big toes,
But, my goodness, what a nose!

Becky Valenick

Bring home the zoo and let your youngster feed his own elephant. Draw a simple elephant's head with big ears and a curving trunk on the side of a box. Make its mouth wide open and smiling. Use a craft knife to cut out the elephant's mouth to make a hole. Let your child toss unshelled peanuts into the elephant's mouth.

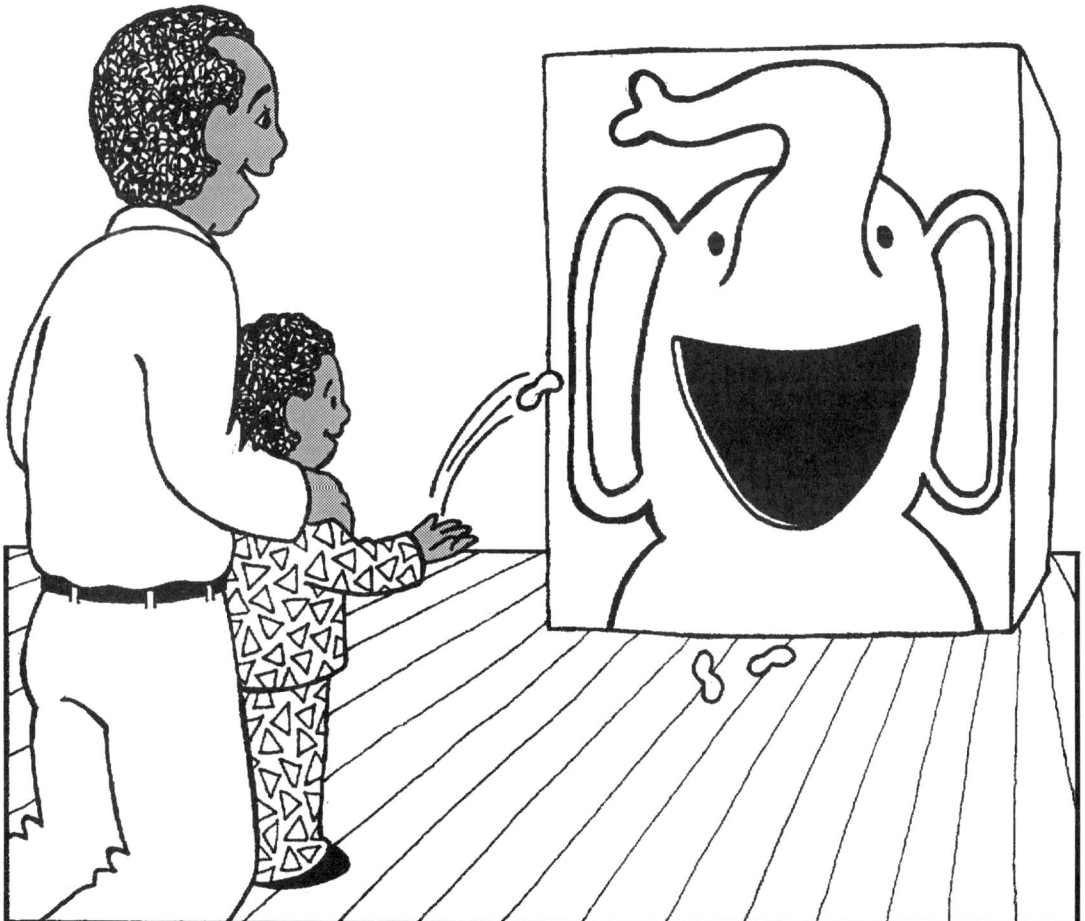

Have You Ever Seen a Camel?

Sung to: "Did You Ever See a Lassie?"

Have you ever seen a camel,
A camel, a camel?
Have you ever seen a camel
With humps on his back?
He walks across sand
In hot desert lands.
Have you ever seen a camel
With humps on his back?

Carla Cotter Skjong

Sing "Have You Ever Seen a Camel?" and let your child pretend to be a camel carrying a heavy load. Wrap a towel around her middle and fasten it with safety pins. Then put a basket on her back and secure it with a belt or rope. Add toys or stuffed animals for cargo as your youngster journeys across the hot desert sand.

A Mighty Lion

Sung to: "If You're Happy and You Know It"

Did you ever hear a mighty lion roar?

Did you ever hear a mighty lion roar?

Oh, a lion roars and roars,

Then he roars and roars some more.

Did you ever hear a mighty lion roar?

Rrrrr!

Debra Lindahl

Share with your child the fact that lions belong to the same family as housecats. After you sing "A Mighty Lion" ask your child to roar like a lion. After singing it a second time, ask him to make the mewing sound of a housecat. How mighty does the lion sound now? What if lions said "meow" and housecats roared?

ROAR!

meow.

How's That Baby?

Sung to: "Clementine"

Kangaroo, kangaroo,
Hopping all about the zoo.
How's that baby in your pocket,
Your baby kangaroo?

He is fine, he is fine,
Always safely tucked inside,
Seeing all there is to see,
Going for a bouncy ride.

Kangaroo, kangaroo,
How you simply love to hop,
Going this way, going that way,
Never taking time to stop.

Susan M. Paprocki

Give your child the experience of caring for her own baby kangaroo. Tie a pouch around her middle, such as a front pack or a soft purse, so it hangs down in front. Let her carry a stuffed animal in her pouch as she hops around. Teach her to sing the middle stanza of "How's That Baby?" as you sing the song with her.

Monkey See, Monkey Do

Sung to: "Jingle Bells"

Monkey see, monkey do
Just the same as you.
If you blink, he will blink.
He will copy you.
Monkey see, monkey do
Just the same as you.
If you blink, he will blink.
He will copy you.

Debra Lindahl

Sharpen your child's observation skills while tickling his funny bone. Sing "Monkey See, Monkey Do" and have him copy you. Continue singing, each time substituting a different action for *blink*. Name funny monkey actions such as *scratch*, *screech*, or *grin*. Take turns with your child being the monkey.

THE OSTRICH

Sung to: "She'll Be Coming Round the Mountain"

Oh, the ostrich is the biggest of the birds.

Oh, the ostrich is the biggest of the birds.

She can run so quickly by,

But she simply cannot fly.

Oh, the ostrich is the biggest of the birds.

Oh, the ostrich lays some big enormous eggs.

Oh, the ostrich lays some big enormous eggs.

Once her baby birds have hatched,

They'll be very hard to catch.

Oh, the ostrich lays some big enormous eggs.

Pat Beck

The next time you are at the grocery store together, show your child how big an ostrich egg is. Find a cantaloupe that is about 6 inches in diameter and weighs about 3 pounds. Let her hold it. Can she imagine a bird's egg that big? At home, point out that ostriches grow to be nearly 8 feet tall, as tall as the ceilings in most houses!

I'm a Little Zebra

Sung to: "I'm a Little Teapot"

I'm a little zebra, black and white.
Hey, don't you think my
Stripes are a sight?
All I like to do is run and play
On the African plains all day.

Jean Warren

Zebras are intriguing to young children because they wear such bold stripes. Increase your child's observation skills by having him look around for other animals or things that have stripes. Are there any stripes on his clothes, bed, or toys? Are there any stripes on your cat? Your child will enjoy drawing some bold stripes with crayons on white paper.

MR. FARMER

Sung to: "Hush, Little Baby"

Mr. Farmer, did you hear
What your cow said in my ear?
Just as plain as plain could be,
She said moo, moo, moo to me.

Durby Peterson

As you sing "Mr. Farmer," substitute other animals and their sounds for *cow* and *moo*. Include such animals as *pig (oink), hen (cluck), horse (neigh), duck (quack),* and *sheep (baa).* Find a picture book with a barnyard scene and let your child point to each animal as you name it. Sing the song again and let her make the animal sounds.

I Like Baby Animals

Sung to: "London Bridge"

I like baby animals,
Animals, animals.
I like baby animals.
I'll name some for you.

Kittens, puppies, chicks, and fawns,
Chicks and fawns, chicks and fawns.
Kittens, puppies, chicks, and fawns.
Can you name some, too?

Bunnies, ducklings, lambs, and cubs,
Lambs and cubs, lambs and cubs.
Bunnies, ducklings, lambs and cubs—
Just to name a few.

Barbara Robinson

Increase your child's matching skills with this game. Select some small index cards. On each card draw or paste a picture of an animal baby such as a kitten, a puppy, a lamb, or a duckling. On additional cards, draw or paste a picture of each baby's mother. Mix up the cards and let your child match up all the babies with their mothers.

AT THE ZOO

Sung to: "Mary Had a Little Lamb"

We are going to the zoo,
To the zoo, to the zoo.
We are going to the zoo.
Oh, won't you please come, too?

We will find some elephants,
Elephants, elephants.
We will find some elephants.
We'll find them at the zoo.

We will find some lions, too,
Lions, too, lions, too.
We will find some lions, too.
We'll find them at the zoo.

Susan M. Paprocki

Animal crackers make this activity a hit. Set out a plate of animal crackers, and as you sing "At the Zoo," have your child look for each animal you name in the song. When she finds the appropriate cookie, let her eat it. Continue singing, substituting the names of the animals left on the plate for the words *elephants* and *lions,* and watch the cookies disappear!

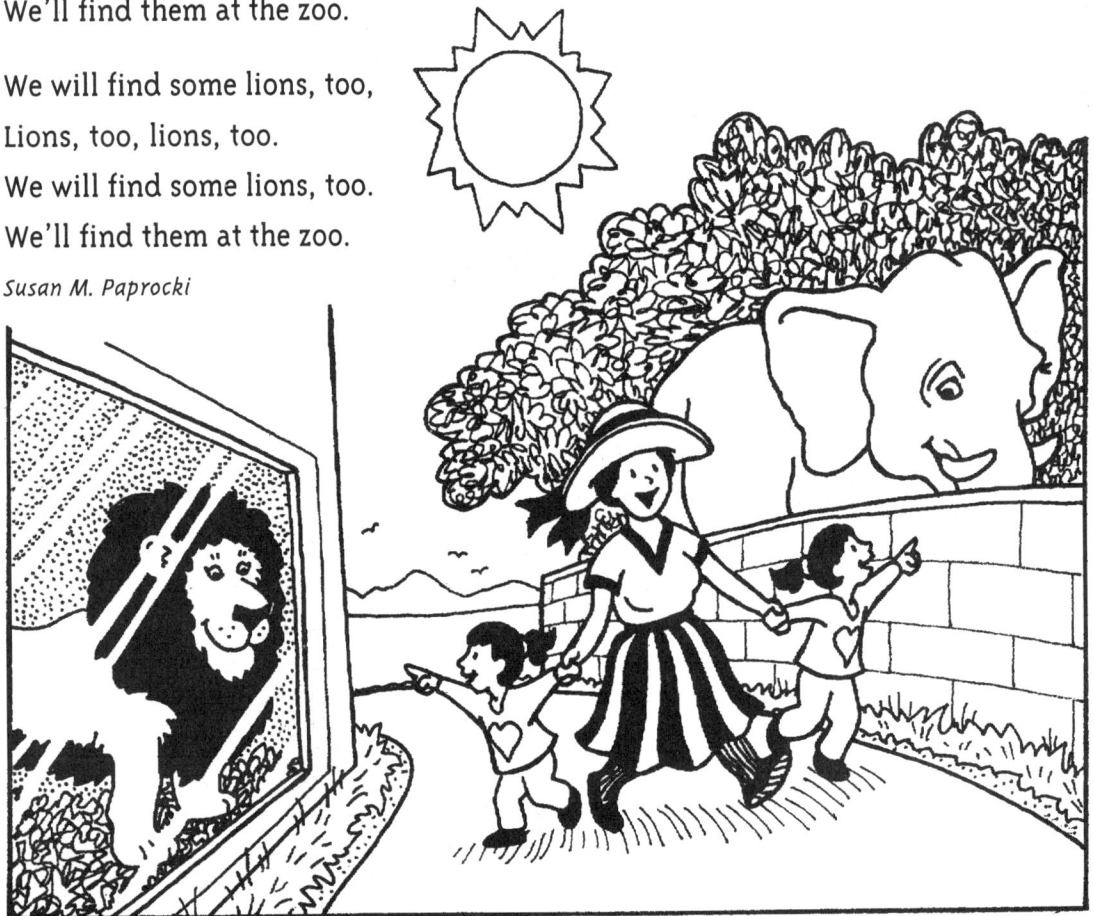

ZOO TRAIN

Sung to: "Rock-a-Bye Baby"

We rode a fun train around the zoo.

Then the animals all wanted rides, too!

A kangaroo sneaked in at the door,

And this is how he got on board.
(Hop like a kangaroo.)

Jean Warren

Be a train engineer and let your child supply the action as you sing "Zoo Train." Lead the train around the room and continue singing, substituting other animals for *kangaroo*. Each time you name an animal, let your child demonstrate how that animal got on board, by hopping, crawling, slithering, and so forth, as the train takes another lap.

THE BEAR

The bear went over the mountain,

The bear went over the mountain,

The bear went over the mountain

To see what he could see.

To see what he could see,

To see what he could see.

The bear went over the mountain,

The bear went over the mountain,

The bear went over the mountain

To see what he could see.

Traditional

Give your child's stuffed bear a starring role. Pile up a pillow mountain and invite your child to make her bear climb up to see all her other stuffed animals on the other side. As you sing "The Bear Went Over the Mountain," let her name which animal the bear sees each time he climbs over the top. Continue singing until the bear has seen them all.

DOWN IN THE OCEAN

Sung to: "Up on the Housetop"

Down in the ocean, far below,

Live many animals that we know.

Fish and crabs and oysters, too,

Swimming free in the ocean blue.

Ho, ho, ho, watch them go.

Some are fast, some are slow.

Down in the ocean, far below,

Live many animals that we know.

Pat Beck

Let your child fish for something to do. Cut some simple fish shapes from construction paper and write an action on each one, such as *crawl like a crab, pucker up like a fish, hug like an octopus,* and so forth. Put the shapes in a bowl. Each time your youngster fishes one out, read the action for him to perform.

Song Index

Parent Resources
from Totline® Publications

A Year of Fun

Hang up these age-specific resource guides for great advice on child development, practical parenting, and age-appropriate activities that jump-start learning.

- **Just for Babies**
- **Just for Ones**
- **Just for Twos**
- **Just for Threes**
- **Just for Fours**
- **Just for Fives**

Beginning Fun With Science

Make science fun for your child with these quick, safe, easy-to-do activities that lead to discovery and spark the imagination.

- **Bugs & Butterflies** • **Plants & Flowers**
- **Magnets** • **Rainbows & Colors**
- **Sand & Shells** • **Water & Bubbles**

Beginning Fun With Art

Perfect for introducing a young child to the fun of art while developing coordination skills and building self-confidence.

- **Scissors** • **Yarn** • **Paint** • **Modeling Dough**
- **Glue** • **Stickers** • **Craft Sticks** • **Crayons** • **Felt**
- **Paper Shapes** • **Rubber Stamps** • **Tissue Paper**

Learning Everywhere

These books present ideas for turning ordinary moments into teaching opportunities. You'll find ways to spend fun, quality time with your child while you lay the foundation for language, art, science, math, problem solving, and building self-esteem.

- **Teaching House**
- **Teaching Town**
- **Teaching Trips**

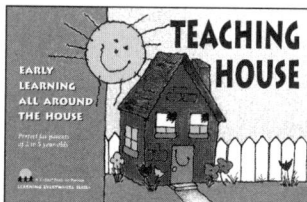

Getting Ready for School

Help your child develop the skills necessary for school success. These activity ideas combine ordinary materials with simple instructions for fun at home that leads to learning.

- **Ready to Learn Colors, Shapes, and Numbers**
- **Ready to Write and Develop Motor Skills**
- **Ready to Read** • **Ready to Communicate**
- **Ready to Listen and Explore the Senses**

Totline books and resources are available at fine teacher and parent stores.

Parent Resources
from Totline® Publications

Seeds for Success

Ideas on how to plant the seeds for success in young children. These parent-friendly books help encourage the development of creativity, responsibility, critical thinking, happiness, and good health. For ages 3 to 5.

- Growing Creative Kids
- Growing Responsible Kids
- Growing Happy Kids
- Growing Thinking Kids

Time to Learn

Now's the time for hands-on learning. Find out how to use low- and no-cost materials to effectively and simply teach your child at home.

- Colors • Letters
- Measuring • Numbers
- Science • Shapes
- Matching and Sorting
- New Words
- Cutting and Pasting
- Drawing and Writing
- Listening
- Taking Care of Myself

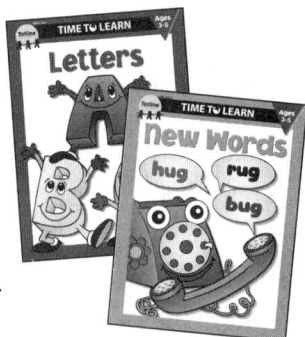

Learn With Piggyback Songs

Children will love to learn age-appropriate themes through music and movement with these delightful song books. Each book has 40 joyful songs and rhymes that help children learn about a specific topic. Plus developmentally appropriate activity ideas extend the learning fun!

- Songs and Games for Babies
- Songs and Games for Toddlers
- Songs and Games for Threes
- Songs and Games for Fours
- Sing a Song of Letters
- Sing a Song of Animals
- Sing a Song of Colors
- Sing a Song of Holidays
- Sing a Song of Me
- Sing a Song of Nature
- Sing a Song of Numbers
- Sing a Song of Shapes

Cassette Tapes

Cassette tapes, featuring selected songs from some of the Learn with Piggyback Songs books, include:

- Songs for Babies
- Songs for Toddlers
- Songs for Threes
- Songs for Fours

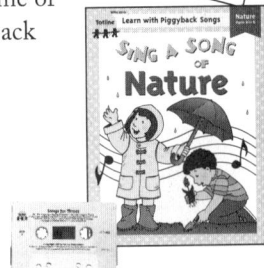

Totline books and resources are available at fine teacher and parent stores.